KEEPING CLEAN

By Slim Goodbody

Photos by Chris Pinchbeck
Illustrations by Ben McGinnis

Consultant: Marlene Melzer-Lange, M.D.
Pediatric Emergency Medicine
Medical College of Wisconsin
Milwaukee, Wisconsin

GARETH**STEVENS**
GS
P U B L I S H I N G
A Member of the WRC Media Family of Companies

Please visit our web site at: www.garethstevens.com
For a free color catalog describing Gareth Stevens Publishing's
list of high-quality books and multimedia programs, call
1-800-542-2595 (USA) or 1-800-387-3178 (Canada).
Gareth Stevens Publishing's fax: (414) 332-3567.

Library of Congress Cataloging-in-Publication Data

Burstein, John.
    Keeping clean / by Slim Goodbody.
       p. cm. — (Slim Goodbody's good health guides)
    Includes bibliographical references and index.
    ISBN-13: 978-0-8368-7742-7 (lib. bdg.)
    1. Hygiene—Juvenile literature. I. Title.
  RA780.B883   2007
  613—dc22   2006032767

This edition first published in 2007 by
Gareth Stevens Publishing
A Member of the WRC Media Family of Companies
330 West Olive Street, Suite 100
Milwaukee, WI 53212 USA

This edition copyright © 2007 by Gareth Stevens, Inc.
Text and artwork copyright © 2006 by Slim Goodbody Corp. (www.slimgoodbody.com).
Slim Goodbody is a registered trademark of Slim Goodbody Corp.

Photos: Chris Pinchbeck, Pinchbeck Photography
Illustrations: Ben McGinnis, Adventure Advertising

Managing editor: Valerie J. Weber
Art direction and design: Tammy West

Printed in Canada

1 2 3 4 5 6 7 8 9 10 10 09 08 07 06

TABLE OF CONTENTS

Words that appear in the glossary are printed in **boldface** type the first time they occur in the text.

Top to Toe

Top to toe
And in between,
You need to keep
Your body clean.
Toothpaste, soap
and hair shampoo
will help to make
a cleaner you.

If you want to look good, smell nice, and stay healthy, you need to keep your whole body clean. That includes your hair, teeth, nails, and all of your skin.

Of course, there is nothing wrong with getting dirty. Life would be really boring if you had to stay clean all the time. You could not jump in puddles, climb trees, or dig holes. You could never play outside.

The problem is not really the dirt. It is the **germs** in the dirt. Germs can make you sick. You cannot see them, but germs are all around you. Every time you touch something or someone, germs are passed along to you. You need to clean these germs away before they can get inside your body and harm you.

Let's learn some ways to keep yourself and the things around you clean.

Something to Think About

There are lots of wonderful things about dirt. It is the home for millions of living things. Plants could not grow without it. Worms, bugs, and even some animals, such as moles, prairie dogs, armadillos, and chipmunks, depend on dirt to build their homes. Unfortunately, germs also like to make their home in dirt.

In Skin

Skin wraps you up from head to toe.
It keeps your insides . . . inside.

Skin also keeps you in touch with the outside world. It lets you feel the wind and rain and the warmth of the sun. It lets you feel a pat on the back, a handshake, and a warm hug.

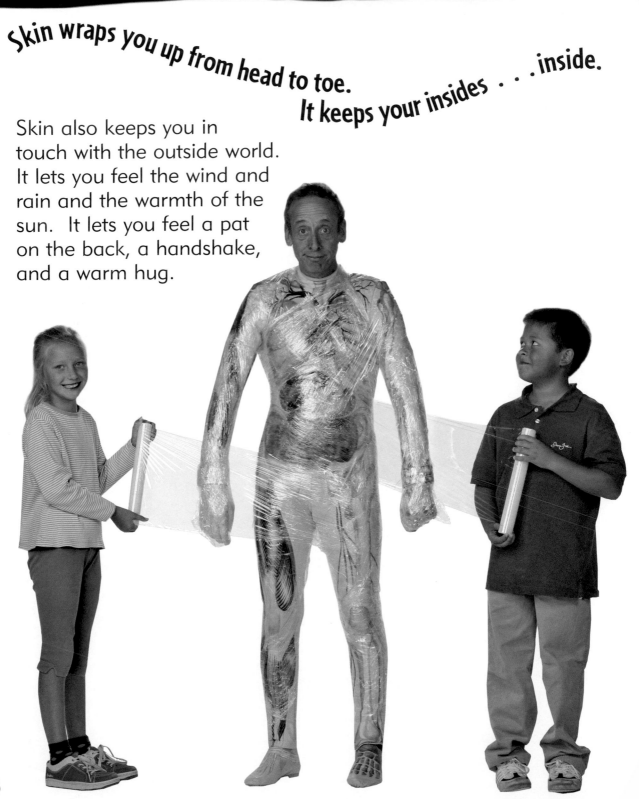

6

Skin is also a great place for germs to collect. There are three reasons for this:

1. You have tiny openings in your skin called pores. These pores release oil, which keeps your skin soft and smooth. The oil also traps germs.

2. Pores release sweat. Sweat helps cool you down when you are hot. Sweat is helpful, except when it stays on your skin too long and starts to smell. When sweat becomes sticky, germs get stuck.

3. Skin fits loosely. Extra skin allows you room to move and grow. Folds and creases are great places for dirt and germs to hide in, however.

If you leave germs on your skin too long, they will start to make you smell bad. They may also find a way to get inside your body and make you sick. They will not go away until you make them.

To get rid of germs, you must wash all over with soap and water.

Something to Think About

Water alone cannot clean away oil. If you have ever washed dirty plates and pans, you know you need dish soap to get rid of the grease. You need soap to get your body clean, too.

Handy Hands

Hands are the greatest tools in the world. Think about all the things they help you do. You use them to carry, catch, throw, tie, push, pull, buckle, button, grab, grasp, pick, pass, and peel. The list could go on and on.

Your hands are busy all day long. They are always in contact with the outside world. They pick up more germs than any other part of your body. If there are germs on your hands and you rub your eyes or put a finger in your mouth or nose, germs can slip inside your body.

Imagine you were playing with worms before dinner and did not wash your hands before your meal. Now, not only are you eating the sandwich you are holding in your hands, but also worm germs and the dirt they live in.

YUCK!

The best way to prevent germs getting into your mouth is to keep your hands clean. You need to wash them:

1. before eating or touching food
2. after using the bathroom
3. after touching pets or other animals
4. after playing outside
5. after visiting a sick relative or friend.

It is not enough just to stick your hands under some running water for a couple of seconds. You must wash correctly. Here is how:

1. Use warm water and any soap you like.
2. Work up a **lather** on both sides of your hands and wrists. Make sure you scrub between your fingers.
3. Do not forget to wash around your nails.
4. Wash for about 15 seconds. If you sing the "A B C" song while washing, that will be enough time to get the germs and dirt off.
5. Rinse the soap off.
6. Dry well with a clean towel.

Something to Think About

Washing your hands can help other people as well. If you wash after blowing your nose or coughing, you will clean away your own germs. Then they cannot get passed on to others.

Scub-A-Dub-Dub

Your body has many bends and turns and small skin folds. There are thousands of places for germs to hide! They might be between your toes or behind your ears. They may have found their way to the backs of your knees, under your arms, or into your bellybutton.

To reach all these places, you need to take a bath or a shower. Then you can get clean all over. Not only will you be washing away the germs, but you will be getting rid of dirt, sweat, oil, and lots of old, dead skin. Many people take a bath or shower every day, but every other day will also do the trick.

Here are some tips for healthy bathing:

1 Before you step into the bath or shower, make sure the water is not too hot. It is easy to get burned.

2 Step in carefully to make sure you do not slip.

3 Use a washcloth. It can help scrub away dirt and germs better than your hands alone can.

4 Remember to wash all over — from your face to your feet.

5 Wrap the washcloth around your finger to clean the outer part of your ear. Do not force anything too far into your ear. If you push too far, you could hurt your **eardrum**.

6 If you take a bath, do not stay in the water after getting clean. If you stay, some of the dirt can float back on you.

Something to Think About

A bath or shower can help in other ways besides cleaning away dirt and germs. A nice bath can be very relaxing after a long day, or a warm shower may wake you up and **jumpstart** your morning. You will look good, feel good, smell good, and be germ free!

Hair Care

When you think of keeping clean, do not forget your hair. The oil that coats your skin also coats your hair. The oil keeps your hair from getting too dry. Dry hair splits and breaks easily. The oil also traps dirt and germs. If you do not keep your hair clean, the oil and dirt will build up. Your hair will feel greasy and look dirty. You do not need to wash your hair as often as you do your body. Washing your hair two times each week should keep it clean and healthy. If you overwash your hair, you can strip away too many oils that keep it soft and smooth.

Here are some hair-washing tips:

1 Before washing, gently comb or brush your hair to get rid of tangles.

2 Using warm water, get your hair all wet.

3 Try to use a shampoo that will not sting your eyes. If you do not have that kind, keep a washcloth nearby to wipe away any shampoo that might get in your eyes.

4 Do not pour shampoo onto your head! It can drip down into your eyes or down your back. Pour a small amount into your palm.

5 Rub your hands together to spread the shampoo evenly.

6 Do not use too much shampoo. If there is not enough lather, your hair probably needs more water, not more shampoo.

7 Really work your fingers on your **scalp** to make sure you reach every hair on your head.

8 Clean all the way down to your scalp.

9 Rinse the soap away completely, or it can leave your hair dry and your scalp feeling itchy.

10 Make sure your hair is dry before going outdoors — especially if it is cool out.

Wet hair + cool air = cold kid

Something to Think About

Between washings, take care of your hair. Brushing or combing regularly helps remove some of the dirt that has collected during the day. Brushing and combing also gets rid of snarls and tangles, so your hair looks nice and neat.

Clip Tips

Fingernails are fine tools. They make it easy to scratch an itch, pull out a splinter, and pick up tiny things.

Fingernails (and toenails) are also a perfect place for germs to hide beneath. As nails grow longer, there is more room for germs to collect. It is also harder to reach underneath the nails to get rid of the germs. Even if you do your best in the bath or shower, it is still important to keep your nails trimmed to the right length.

14

Here are some clip tips:

1 When your nails start catching on things, it is time for action.

2 Ask your parents for help. Clippers and scissors are sharp.

3 Do not cut your nails too short. That can hurt!

4 Trim your nails straight across but round the edges a little.

5 Once they are trimmed, use a nail file or **emery board** to smooth any rough spots.

There are other good reasons for keeping your nails trimmed:

1 You will have less chance of breaking or bending a nail, which can be very painful.

2 You will be less likely to accidentally scratch something or someone else.

3 There will be less chance of biting your nails or picking at them, which can sometimes lead to **infections**.

Something to Think About

Toenails grow more slowly than fingernails. They do not need to be trimmed as often as fingernails do.

Tooth Talk

When you look in the mirror and smile, you see your nice, white teeth. You do not see the **plaque** there as well.

Plaque is a clear film that coats your teeth. It is very sticky. Plaque traps germs and tiny bits of food. The germs use these food bits to make an **acid**. This acid eats away at your tooth and, after a while, can cause a **cavity**.

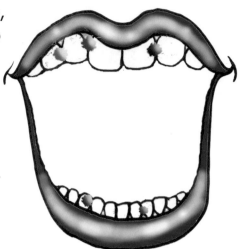

Plaque can also cause gum disease and bad breath. To get rid of plaque, you need to brush and **floss** every day. Brushing removes plaque from the large areas of your teeth and from just under your gums. Flossing removes plaque from between your teeth.

Here is what you need to do to keep your teeth and gums healthy:

1 Floss once a day. Take your time and do not rush.

2 Brush at least twice a day — in the morning after breakfast and in the evening just before going to bed.

3 Do not brush more than three times a day. A third brushing after lunch or a snack can help, but too much brushing can actually hurt your gums.

4 Always use a toothbrush with soft or extrasoft bristles. If the bristles are too hard, they can hurt your gums. You can also use an electric toothbrush instead.

5 Make sure you have the right-sized toothbrush. A brush that is too small will not do a good job. A brush that is too big might hurt your mouth.

6 Change your toothbrush when the bristles begin to spread out. Usually you need a new toothbrush about every three months.

7 Be sure to visit the dentist once a year.

Something to Think About

The hardest part of your body is the **enamel** coating on your teeth. It is even harder than bone. Without your help, however, it cannot stop germs from causing cavities.

Brushing Basics

Your teeth do many things for you. They chew food, help you speak, and make your face look nice. Now that you know how important it is to keep your teeth clean, it is time to learn how to do the job really well.

To brush:

1 Only use a small amount of toothpaste — about the size of a pea. Too much paste makes too much foam, and you cannot see what you are doing.

2 Tilt the brush head so the bristles can reach the place where your teeth meet your gums. You want the bristles to clean the sides of your teeth AND the space between your teeth and gums. A lot of plaque builds up in those places.

3 Move the brush in small circles. Make sure you brush every tooth well.

4 Brush lightly. Brushing too hard can hurt your gums.

5 Brush the back of your teeth as well as the front.

6 Turn the toothbrush straight up and down to brush the insides of your front teeth.

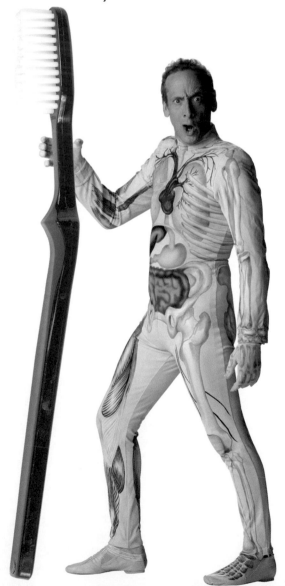

7 Brush the biting and chewing part of your teeth by holding the bristles straight down on the flat area. Use a back-and–forth motion.

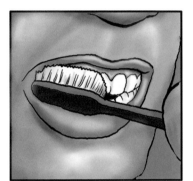

8 Brush all of your teeth.

9 Brush your teeth in the same order each time. It does not matter which tooth gets brushed first or last, but if you do it the same way each day, you will not forget a tooth.

10 Brush for 2 minutes or longer. You cannot clean all your teeth properly in less time.

11 Spit out the toothpaste when you are finished. Do not swallow it. Then rinse your mouth with cool water.

Something to Think About

Do not forget to brush your tongue. It cleans away germs that can give you bad breath. Use your toothbrush to brush your tongue gently from back to front. Do not go too far back in your mouth or you might gag. When you are done, rinse your mouth clean.

Boss of the Floss

Flossing is just as important as brushing. Most cavities are found between your teeth in tight places where a toothbrush cannot reach. The floss gets rid of food that is hidden where your toothbrush cannot reach, no matter how well you brush.

Learning to floss takes time and practice. When you first get started, ask the dentist or your parents to show you how to do it right.

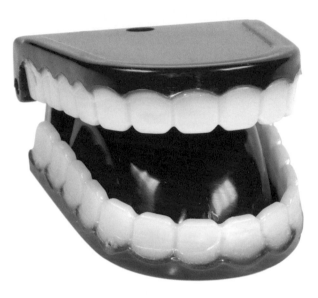

1 Use a piece of floss about 12 to 18 inches (30 to 46 centimeters) long.

2 Wrap the ends around your middle fingers, leaving about 2 inches (5 cm) of floss between them.

3 Guide the floss with your index fingers. You can also wind it around your index fingers and guide it with your thumb and middle fingers or use a floss-guiding tool.

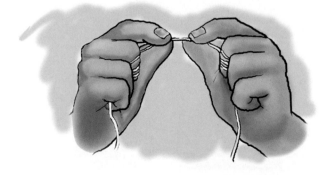

4 Slowly work the floss into the space between two teeth.

5 If the fit is tight, use a gentle back-and-forth motion to work the floss through the narrow spot.

6 Do not snap the floss into place quickly or you could cut your gums

7 Curve the floss around each tooth in a C shape. Gently move it up and down the side of each tooth. Include the space just under the gum line.

8 Do not rub too hard or you might injure your gums. You want to rub just hard enough to skim off the plaque in that area.

9 Floss all sides of the tooth.

10 Use a clean part of the floss for each tooth.

Something to Think About

Flossing and brushing are only a part of keeping healthy teeth. You also need to be careful about what you eat and drink. Try to avoid foods with lots of sugar and foods that are sticky. Eat healthy snacks — lots of fruits and vegetables — and drink water instead of soda.

Shirt Dirt

Have you ever smelled your shirt at the end of a long and active day? It can smell pretty stinky. Every day, your body sweats, releases oil, and you shed millions of dead skin cells. The oil and cells get on the clothes you wear. So do germs.

Even if the shirt and pants you wore yesterday look clean, they actually have invisible dirt and germs on them. It may be fine to wear them a couple of more times if they do not look dirty.

Soon, however, they will need to be washed.

Underpants are a different story. No matter how careful you are, underpants pick up germs when you go to the bathroom. Even if they look clean, underpants should be changed everyday.

Another thing that needs to be washed is your sheets. Chances are, you run around barefoot before you get into bed. If there is dirt on the floor, it gets onto your foot. Next thing you know, it is on your sheets. Your pillowcase does not stay clean for long either. Even if you wash your face before bed, you probably do not shampoo your hair every night. Dirt, oil, and germs from your face and hair find their way onto your pillowcase.

Towels also need to be cleaned. No matter how well you wash your hands or body, a little dirt or a few germs remain. Some of these rub off on to the towels you use to dry yourself.

Something to Think About

Clothes, sheets, pillowcases, and towels will not clean themselves. They must be washed with water and soap. You can help do the laundry. Here is how:

1. Collect your dirty clothes in a basket or pile.
2. Empty all your pockets of coins, tissues, gum, paper, or anything else.
3. Carry clothes, sheets, pillowcases, and towels to the washing machine on laundry day.
4. When the washing and drying is done, help match your socks in pairs.
5. Help fold and put away your clothes.

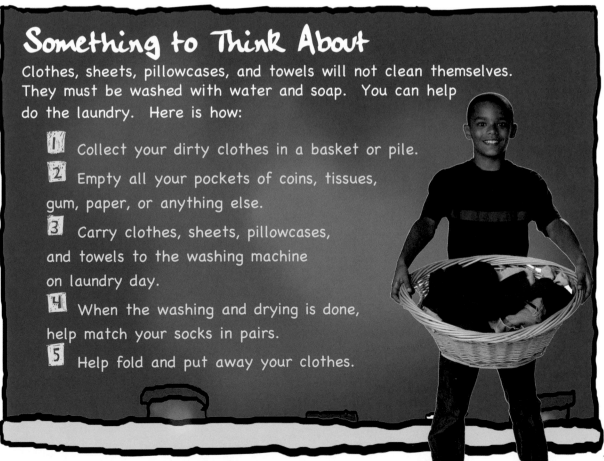

Home, Clean Home

You spend lots of time at home, so it is a good idea to keep it clean. You can help your parents with this important job in many ways. You can vacuum the floors or dust the furniture. You can also pick up any trash you find and put it into the garbage.

Here are some other things you can do:

In your bedroom:

1. Tidy up. A messy room can hide a lot of dirt and germs. You never know what you may find growing in that big pile of laundry in the corner!

2. Put away your toys. If your toys are off the floor, they will not get as dirty.

In the kitchen:

1 Make sure your plates, spoons, forks, knives, and glasses are clean before you eat.

2 After you have eaten, carry your dishes to the sink.

3 Wipe the table to clean away any leftover foods.

4 Ask your parents if you can help wash the dishes.

In the bathroom:

1 Flush the toilet after using it.

2 If the sink is dirty after you wash your hands, run some extra water and clean it. Then be sure to wash your hands again with soap.

3 If you play with toys in the bathtub, put them away to dry when you are done.

Something to Think About

The food you eat should be clean, too. Cooking kills germs. If you eat raw vegetables or fruits, be sure to wash them well before taking a bite.

Pollution Solution

We share our world with every other living thing — every animal and plant on the planet. Human beings make a lot of garbage and **pollution**, which is unhealthy for everyone. It is a big problem, but there are ways you can help.

Here is how:

REDUCE
That means to buy less and use less. The truth is that many of us have lots of stuff we do not need. Sometimes we buy something just because our friends have it or ads on television make it look cool. If we reduce what we buy, we will reduce the garbage we make. So buy only what you need and use what you buy.

REUSE
That means to use something more than once. For example, when you get a plastic bag, use it again the next time you go shopping. Instead of ripping the gift paper off presents, take it off carefully. Then you can use it again. When something breaks, fix it instead of throwing it away. New is not always better.

RECYCLE
That means to remake something into something new. Just about anything in your home or school that cannot be reused can be recycled into something else. For example, scrap paper from your notebook might be turned into newspaper or paper bags. A recycled soda bottle can be made into

fleeces, combs, or hundreds of other plastic products that can be used for many years.

DO NOT LITTER

If you have a used tissue or a candy or gum wrapper, throw it in the trash can where it belongs. Never toss garbage on the street or into a stream or lake. At home, make sure that garbage can lids are on tightly so no garbage can fall or get blown out.

Something to Think About

Smoke in the air can dirty your lungs and maybe make you sick. If you see somebody smoking, do not get too close. Your lungs deserve the best care — fresh air.

A Clean Scene

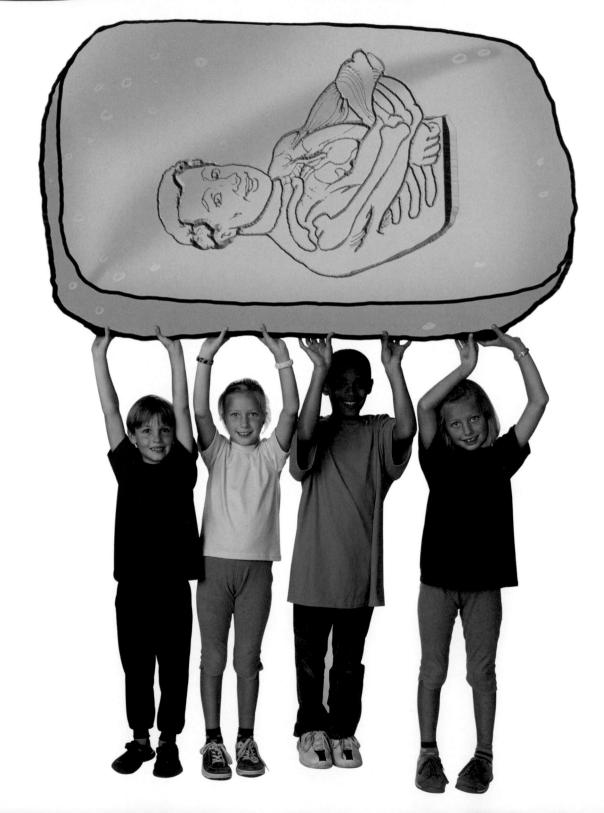

Now you know where germs are found,
So do not let them hang around.
Exercise your cleaning power
In the bathtub or the shower.
Wash your hands, so no germ lingers
Hiding out between your fingers.
Brush and floss your teeth each day,
So germs cannot cause tooth decay.
Wash your clothes in the machine
That spins them round and makes them clean.
Toss litter in the garbage can
And keep our planet spic and span.

Something to Think About

When you keep yourself and your **environment** clean, you are setting a good example for others to follow. As more people do their part, the world will become a cleaner and healthier place to live in.

Glossary

acid — harsh chemicals that can break solids apart

cavity — a hole in a tooth

eardrum — the thin layer that separates the outer and middle ear and carries sound waves to the tiny bones in the middle ear

emery board — a nail file made of cardboard covered with a dark, grainy polishing mineral

enamel — the thin, hard layer on the surface of teeth

environment — the entire surroundings in which we live

floss — to use a special waxed or plastic thread to clean between the teeth

germs — tiny living things that can often cause diseases

infections — sicknesses or diseases caused by germs

jumpstart — to get something going quickly

lather — foam formed when soap is rubbed, stirred, or shaken in water

plaque — a sticky film on teeth that contains germs

pollution — dirt or unwanted chemicals in the earth, air, or water

scalp — the top of the head usually covered with hair

For More Information

BOOKS

Healthy Body: Personal Hygiene. Healthy Body (series).
   Carol Ballard (Blackbirch Press)

No B.O.!: The Head-to-Toe Book of Hygiene for Preteens.
   Marguerite Crump (Free Spirit Publishing)

Personal Hygiene. Reading Essentials in Science: Healthy Living
   (series). Alexandra Powe Allred (Perfection Learning)

Personal Hygiene and Good Health. Living Well, Staying Healthy
   (series). Shirley Wimbish Gray (Child's World)

Personal Hygiene?: What's That Got To Do With Me? Pat Crissey
   and Noah Crissey (Jessica Kingsley Publishers)

WEB SITES

American Dental Association's Animations and Game Pages
www.ada.org/public/games/index.asp
Click on the links to learn more about proper brushing and flossing.

BAM! Body and Mind
www.bam.gov/sub_yourbody/yourbody_smilestyle.html
This site from the Centers for Disease Control and Prevention helps
you learn more about taking care of your teeth. Play games and
take quizzes on dental health.

Slim Goodbody
www.slimgoodbody.com
Discover loads of fun and free downloads for kids and parents.

Note to educators and parents: The publisher has carefully reviewed these Web
sites to ensure that they are suitable for children. Many Web sites change frequently,
however, and Gareth Stevens, Inc., cannot guarantee that a site's future contents
will continue to meet our high standards of quality and educational value. Be
advised that children should be closely supervised whenever they access the Internet.

Index

About the Author

John Burstein (also known as Slim Goodbody) has been entertaining and educating children for over thirty years. His programs have been broadcast on CBS, PBS, Nickelodeon, USA, and Discovery. Over the years, he has developed programs with the American Association for Health Education, the American Academy of Pediatrics, the National YMCA, the President's Council on Physical Fitness and Sports, the International Reading Association, and the National Council of Teachers of Mathematics. He has won numerous awards including the Parent's Choice Award and the President's Council's Fitness Leader Award. Currently, Mr. Burstein tours the country with his multimedia live show "Bodyology." For more information, please visit slimgoodbody.com.